White poppies

A PLAY BY SUE SAUNDERS

www.heinemann.co.uk

✓ Free online support
✓ Useful weblinks
✓ 24 hour online ordering

01865 888008

Heinemann is an imprint of Pearson Education Limited, a company incorporated in England and Wales, having its registered office at Edinburgh Gate, Harlow, Essex, CM20 2JE. Registered company number: 872828

www.heinemann.co.uk

Heinemann is a registered trademark of Pearson Education Limited

Text © Heinemann 2008

First published 2008

12 11
10 9 8 7 6 5

British Library Cataloguing in Publication Data
A catalogue record for this book is available from the British Library

ISBN 978 0 435233 45 7

Typeset by Phoenix Photosetting, Chatham, Kent, UK
Printed in China (CTPS/05)

'Your lives have been blessed by the opportunity to learn; you have been schooled, and each one of you has benefited from this knowledge, proportionate to your own intellect. Now is the time to use these years of learning to help shape your own fortune. Set yourself goals and targets. Be positive – start today to think where you would like to be next year. Don't aim too high – always work within your own capability. The best of luck to you all.'

Henry Allingham, July 2006, Age 110

Mr Allingham was one of the handful of World War I veterans still alive in 2006. He was contacted through Denis Goodwin of the Veterans' Association, who helped Henry to write this dedication, addressed to today's students.

Contents

Teaching resources

To help deliver the questions and activities on pages 71–82, teaching materials are available to download free from www.heinemann.co.uk/literature

---

Websites

These are links to relevant websites in this book. In order to ensure that the links are up to date, that the links work, and that the sites are not inadvertently linked to sites that could be considered offensive, we have made the links available on the Heinemann website at www.heinemann.co.uk/hotlinks. When you access the site, the express code is 3457.

Cast list

Characters from the present day
Mrs Clark
Jenny Clark, (14) *her daughter*
Two teachers at Jenny's school
Other students at Jenny's school

Characters from 1914/1915
Jenny Lucas, (15)
Hannah Lucas/Clark, (18) *her sister*
Mattie Clark, (18) *Hannah's husband*
Tom Hedley, (16) *Mattie's best friend*
Mrs Hedley, *Tom's mother*
Will Fordham, (19) *a gentleman*
Lord Fordham, *Will's father*
Polly Watkins, (17) *a kitchen maid*
Lizzie Palmer, (17) *a kitchen maid*
The Vicar of Byford Church
Dr Lindsay, *the local doctor*
Milkman
Recruiting Officer
Corporal, *a corporal in Tom and Mattie's regiment*
Captain Knox, *a captain in Tom and Mattie's regiment*
An NCO *(Non-Commissioned Officer)*
Mr Hines, the Orderly
Major Henderson, *a major in Tom and Mattie's regiment*
General villagers

Characters from 1941
Jenny Lucas/Hedley, (42)
Hannah Clark, (45)
John Clark, (26) *Hannah's son*

Act One

Scene 1

June, 1914

Outside. An early summer evening. Background sounds of country dance music, and of people enjoying themselves. Enter Jenny Lucas and the Milkman. Both wear outdoor clothes. Both are laden with baggage.

MILKMAN   There you are, **lass**. Here's yer bags. *(he puts them down)*

JENNY L   Thank you! *(she puts down the bags she was carrying)*

MILKMAN   Sounds **champion** in there!

JENNY L   Would anybody mind if you came and joined in for a bit?   5

MILKMAN   Well then, lass, I don't suppose they would. But I think the horse would take a dim view of it! Long past his bedtime, it is. And we're up to fetch the milk from the dairy at six in the morning! I'll be needing to get Charlie   10 there back to the stable sharpish.

JENNY L   I'll need to give you some money ... *(she fumbles in her purse)* ... oh dear, I don't know what—

MILKMAN   Never you mind that. The mistress will settle up with me in the morning. She's right glad   15 of some extra help in the house, I reckon. Otherwise she wouldn't have sent me to seek you at the station. Bye, lass. See you around, no doubt.

JENNY L Bye! *(the milkman leaves as Hannah, in bridal finery, now slightly dishevelled, comes running in)* 20

HANNAH Jenny! There you are!

JENNY L Hannah! Oh, it's good to see you! *(they embrace)*

HANNAH I was worried about you getting off the train in the dark all by yerself.

JENNY L Well the **cabbie** was really nice. He was 25 shining his lamp up and down the platform to find me. And he had this big notice saying 'Jenny – for Byford Hall', so I knew he'd come for me!

HANNAH He's not really a cabbie you know. He's Bob the milkman and he's the only one around 30 here with a cart! My little sister! I can't believe you're so tall in just six months!

JENNY L And I can't believe you're married. Let's see the ring. *(she examines Hannah's left hand)* Oh! That's lovely. I do wish I'd been here for the 35 wedding. I'm really sorry I wasn't. It was only yesterday we got the new girl to help out in the shop.

HANNAH We both know Auntie couldn't do without you – don't worry. It's just good to see you here 40 for the dancing.

Mattie and Tom enter. Tom stands back while Mattie comes to hold Hannah's hand.

HANNAH Mattie! Here's Jenny!

MATTIE She's told me a lot about you. Hello, Jenny.

JENNY L Are they really holding a special dance just for you? Even though you're just servants?

MATTIE   Not quite! The party's for Master Will. He's   45
off to college soon. But Master and Mistress
said we could have our friends along to join
in, 'cos of the wedding. Come on, sweetheart,
time for the last dance. Jenny, here's me pal,
Tom Hedley. He'll be yer partner.   50

TOM   Hello.

JENNY L   I don't know as I can dance like you do here!

TOM   Don't worry. Enjoy yerself!

*The four young people '**honour**' their partners for
the country dance, as the music and background
murmuring swells to suggest a roomful of people
taking part in the dance. Exit Tom, Jenny Lucas,
Mattie and Hannah.*

Scene 2

The present day

*The Clarks' kitchen. Jenny Clark arrives home from
school, takes off her tie, flings it on the ground,
starts to eat a biscuit. She takes off her jacket,
gets out her phone and dials.*

JENNY C   Hi, Sarah. How are you feeling? Drowning in
tissues? … Oh good! You'll be back on
Monday then – just in time for the Maths test
… Well, just thought I'd warn you! … No,
you didn't miss much in Games …   5
Don't think so, just revising for the test and
reading the book for English. Oh, there was
one thing. And I suppose you might feel like
thinking about it in your *(with exaggerated
solemnity)* '**prostrate**' state …   10

MRS CLARK	*(offstage)* Hi, Jenny! *(Mrs Clark enters, laden with bags)*
JENNY C	Hi Mum … Are you still there? Yes, just Mum coming in. What was I saying? Oh yes, it's for History. It's a sort of project about the First World War … No, not **the Blitz**, idiot, that was the second one. The First World War, when the ***Titanic*** sank.
MRS CLARK	Nothing to do with the *Titanic*!
JENNY C	Shut up, Mum! … Yes, well we've got to find out about what our families might have been doing in 1914, you know, if they fought any battles or anything. And then there's going to be a ceremony at school on **Poppy Day**. And we're going to read out everybody's names – the ancestors, I mean – and sing songs and have poems … yeah, sounds quite good. It'll get us off double Games in winter, anyway! So I thought you could start thinking about it … Right, OK! See you Monday, or Tuesday if you want to give the Maths test a miss! *(she switches off her phone)*
MRS CLARK	Sounds interesting!
JENNY C	It's better than old Harry's usual ideas anyway! Have we got any stuff about great granddads and grandmas and so on?
MRS CLARK	Probably, but just now I can't think of anything but a cup of tea.
JENNY C	Righto!
MRS CLARK	What are you up to this weekend, apart from researching your ancestors?

15

20

25

30

35

40

JENNY C   *(ticking off imaginary items on her fingers)* Buying
a present for Lisa's birthday, going to the
party on Saturday, deciding what to wear for
going to the party, washing my hair for going
to the party … oh, and having a long lie   45
in after the party – till eleven at least!

MRS CLARK   Eleven! Just think yourself lucky *you* weren't
your great granny – you'd have had to be up
at six every day, rain or shine, weekend or no
weekend.   50

Exit Jenny Clark and Mrs Clark.

Scene 3

September, 1914

*Outside Byford Hall. Jenny Lucas enters, yawning.
She has a basket of peas, which she sits down to
shell. Tom enters with a parcel.*

TOM   Is that you, Jenny?

JENNY L   Oh, hello, Tom. I was dozing over the peas.

TOM   Peas? *(comes over to look)* Oh, I see.

JENNY L   Cook said I could sit out here in the sun and
shell them, just for a bit of fresh air. I'm   5
not quite used to being in the kitchen all the
time, and none of the other lasses will talk to
me yet!

TOM   I'll help if you like.

JENNY L   Oh, thanks! Anyway, what're you doing here?   10

TOM   Mam sent me down with stuff from our shop –
sweets and biscuits for Master Will going
away to fight. He got a place at the big

15

university down in Cambridge you know,
but he decided to join the army instead.

JENNY L He must be right clever! Is he going straight out
to France?

TOM No, training first – in the big army camp near
Lakely. Maybe the war'll be all over before he
gets there.

20

JENNY L They said it'll be done by Christmas.

TOM Right enough. *(pause)* Lakely's where you and
Hannah come from, isn't it?

JENNY L Yes. *(pause)* Why does yer mam send Master
Will sweets and things?

25

TOM It's a sort of thank you. 'Cos he's always lending
me books. He said he'd some to give me
today before he goes to the camp.

JENNY L How are you and him friendly? With him
being one of the big house – and you just
a shop lad?

30

TOM Mam and me helped him save a fox from the
hunt.

JENNY L A fox?

TOM Master Will isn't yer normal sort of upper
class **gent**. In fact, I honestly don't know how
he'll make out in the army. He hates fox
hunting – thinks it's cruel.

35

JENNY L Yes, but how did you all save a fox?

TOM It was about a year ago. Mam and me were
clearing up outside the shop …

40

*Tom exits. Jenny moves to the side of the stage to
watch the following 'flashback'.*

Scene 4

September, 1913

Outside the Hedleys' shop/cottage and shed. Mrs Hedley enters, sweeping. Enter Will, as if shooing something before him into the shed.

WILL   Go, go, go … that's right, in you go. Now then …

MRS HEDLEY   Oh, Master Will is it? From the Hall? You gave me a fright.

WILL   Sorry Mrs … Mrs …

MRS HEDLEY   Hedley.   5

WILL   Yes – well, Mrs Hedley, I was wondering if you had any ginger beer to sell. Thirsty work this riding!

MRS HEDLEY   Well, yes, surely. Won't you come inside then? *(sound of hunting horns)*

WILL   Could you possibly bring it out here?   10

MRS HEDLEY   Yes, I could, but … is there something in that coal shed?

WILL   A fox! A very frightened fox. *(Tom enters, Will looks at Tom)* Would you help me hide it?

TOM   There's no lock on that door.   15

WILL   I know, that's why I'm standing in front of it.

TOM   But the hounds will soon be after it.

WILL   I don't think so – I've just thrown a few kippers at them – that should put them off the scent! Oh, no, here's Father.   20

Lord Fordham enters.

LORD FORDHAM   Will – what on earth are you doing here! We seem to have lost the scent. Why aren't you

mounted? We need every man we can
muster if we're to get on to this wretched
fox again.   25

WILL   I got thrown down by Longacres Wood, Father.
My wrist's a bit sore. I think I'll just walk back
home; Dusty will make her own way back,
I'm sure. She's a good **mare**.

LORD FORDHAM   I'm sure she will. She's more sense than   30
you have sometimes. *(to Tom and Mrs Hedley)*
Good day to you! *(he exits)*

WILL   Well, that's all very satisfactory! I'll be off then –
would you mind very much seeing the fox
gets off safely?   35

Scene 5

September, 1914

*Outside Byford Hall. Jenny Lucas walks forward
towards Tom.*

JENNY L   I like that! He sounds **grand**! Those books he
lends you – are you much of a reader then?

TOM   Suppose so. I feel a bit daft saying this, but I'd
really like to be a teacher when I'm older.

JENNY L   Doesn't it cost lots to be a teacher?   5

TOM   I'm going to the Grammar School this year. Mr
Mariner, the head teacher, says I've a chance
of the training college after that.

JENNY L   But doesn't it still cost lots?

TOM   Well, I was lucky – I got a scholarship.   10
There's three of us going to the Grammar.

| JENNY L | I'd have loved to go on to grammar school but I had to leave when I was fourteen to help our auntie. She's got a shop as well, down Lakely way. It's a draper's. | 15 |

TOM   What about yer mam and dad?

JENNY L   Mam's dead.

TOM   Oh – oh, I'm sorry.

JENNY L   That's all right. It happened a long time ago. She died when I was born. Dad was 20 from Ireland and he went back home to be with me nana and grandpa for a while. He met somebody else while he was back there and married her. He sent for me and Hannah to go over, but Auntie wrote to him that 25 we'd be better off with her. She's got no family of her own. And she's been grand.

TOM   Well, I've got no dad. He was a miner, and he was killed in a big **pit** explosion when I was seven. 30

JENNY L   That must have been terrible for yer mam.

TOM   I think it's one reason why she's so keen for me to go to the Grammar School. She certainly doesn't want me to go down the mine like me dad! 35

Will enters with a parcel. He is wearing his uniform.

TOM   I didn't recognise you. Very posh!

WILL   It feels two sizes too big in some places and two sizes too small in others! Who … ? *(he indicates Jenny)*

TOM   This is Jenny. She's sister-in-law to me pal, Mattie.

WILL	Oh yes! I haven't seen you before, have I?	40

JENNY L I've just come here, sir. I'm from Lakely and me sister Hannah – she's the one that's just got married to Mattie, Tom's pal, – she's yer mam's – I mean Lady Fordham's – parlour maid.

WILL And are you working in the house too? 45

JENNY L I'm in the kitchen. Oh dear … *(Jenny's name is shouted several times. She picks up the basket of peas guiltily. Lizzie enters)*

LIZZIE Cook says you're to come straight away.

JENNY L Sorry.

Tom and Will exchange parcels.

LIZZIE 'Cos Cook says you're taking advantage.

JENNY L Advantage? 50

LIZZIE Of being a spoilt brat and getting treats just 'cos yer sister's a chamber maid.

JENNY L Well I never meant to …

LIZZIE **Mebbes not**, but the rest of us don't like it, see! So just you watch out. *(Lizzie exits)* 55

JENNY L I'd better go. Goodbye, Tom. Goodbye, sir.

TOM AND WILL Goodbye. *(Jenny walks away. Tom runs after her. Will looks in his parcel and starts to munch a biscuit)*

TOM *(to Jenny)* If you'd like to come and see us at the shop some Sunday when you have a day's holiday … ? Mam loves making special teas. 60

JENNY L Oooh – that'd be lovely. Thank you, Tom! Reckon Hannah's going to be too busy being married for a few weeks to be much company.

TOM	Just send word up and I'll come and seek you.
JENNY L	Bye! *(Jenny exits)* 65
TOM	*(to Will, who is still eating biscuits)* You'll have those all eaten before you get away!
WILL	Hope you like the books. There's some maps and geometry, and some history, and a few novels. Oh, and a bit of poetry if you like 70 that sort of thing.
TOM	Now and then. You've marked some of them.
WILL	Yes! How's this for stirring stuff? *(he reads)* 'Out of the night that covers me 75 Black as the pit from pole to pole, I thank whatever gods may be For my unconquerable soul ...'

Will and Tom laugh and exit together.

Scene 6

The present day

Jenny Clark and Mrs Clark come in. They have a small trunk out of which they take various papers and notebooks, and a similar book to the one Will has been reading. Jenny reads aloud from it.

JENNY C	'... it matters not how **strait** the gate, How charged with punishment the scroll, I am the master of my fate I am the keeper of my soul ...' *(to her mother)* It sounds a bit like a hymn 5 or something!
MRS CLARK	Very British Empire!

JENNY C	Why didn't you show me any of this stuff before?

MRS CLARK   Well, just remember how little you were when
your dad died … We hadn't been married   10
long, he was an only child and his own mum
and dad had died a few years earlier. Men
can be hopeless about their family history,
you know – just like they are at remembering
birthdays. The only thing I *do* know is   15
that Roger wanted your name to be 'Jenny
Hedley Clark' – just like his was 'Roger
Hedley Clark' – after an old family friend.
And, of course, he had that trunk.

JENNY C   Why did you never look in it?   20

MRS CLARK   I think at the time your dad died I felt it would
have made me too sad. Well, he wouldn't
have been there for me to ask him about the
things in it – and then, to be honest, I just
forgot about it. It's nice seeing *you* looking   25
through it, though!

JENNY C   What would have happened if you hadn't liked
'Jenny' for a name?

MRS CLARK   Lucky I did or there might have been a row!
I was a bit doubtful about the 'Hedley'   30
bit, but it sounded very dignified and
I thought you might end up being Prime
Minister some day – Lady Jenny Hedley Clark!

Jenny throws a cushion at her.

JENNY C   Well, I'm going to read all this lot and try to
find out why I've got landed with 'Hedley'.   35
Everyone in my class has middle names they
can use if they get fed up with their first

names. Like Sara's middle name is Claire and
she writes Zara with a 'Z' and Clair without
the 'E' all over her books. I'd look pretty   40
silly writing 'Hedley Clark', wouldn't I?

MRS CLARK *(getting something from the trunk)* Whose is this
tin, do you think?

JENNY C Let's see … It's got a name on, and a date …
Edward Hedley, 1900, Byford Pit. There   45
isn't a pit at Byford, is there?

MRS CLARK I think there used to be – it's all covered over
now. I think I read once that there was a big
explosion there, not long after 1900.

JENNY C Was Edward Hedley a relation?   50

MRS CLARK I keep telling you, love – I really don't know.
Sorry. We'll just have to see if there's
anything else in the trunk that gives us a clue.

Exit Jenny Clark and Mrs Clark.

Scene 7

October, 1914

*Inside the Hedleys' kitchen. Mrs Hedley, Tom and
Jenny Lucas are seated; Mrs Hedley is knitting.
Tom is showing Jenny a box identical to the one in
the present day.*

TOM This is me dad's **bait box** – for when he went
down the mine.

MRS HEDLEY His name's on it. That's how they knew him
when they brought him out of the pit – he
was that badly cut about.   5

JENNY L I'm sorry, Mrs Hedley.

MRS HEDLEY	Life goes on, lass. Have you got keepsakes from yer mam?
JENNY L	This – it's me mam's hair in the locket. *(she shows Mrs Hedley)*
MRS HEDLEY	That's nice.

10

TOM	What about yer dad? I know he's not dead, like, but Ireland's a long way off.
JENNY L	He writes twice a year. He's not much of a scholar, mind. I think me stepmam puts down what he wants to say.

15

TOM	Yer mam must have been the scholar then. 'Cos you're clever.
JENNY L	But I don't know half as much as you. What with leaving school early, and all.
MRS HEDLEY	Don't run yerself down, lass. Book learning's not everything.

20

TOM	Mam, have you got that stuff for Jenny to fetch back? Then I'll walk with her down the lane to wait for the pony and **trap** – Dr Lindsay'll be setting off for **evensong** soon.

25

MRS HEDLEY	Here it is. *(hands over two small parcels)* Some treats for you and some for that sister of yours – she looked **out of sorts** last time I saw her in the village.
JENNY	*(confidentially to Mrs Hedley – Tom is putting away the bait tin)* She's not out of sorts – she's expecting a **bairn**!

30

MRS HEDLEY	Is she now! Then I expect Mattie'll have told Tom so you've no need to whisper! They're **thick as thieves**, those two. Right, Tom? Come straight

back now – no **hanky panky**! See you on   35
yer half day next week if you like, Jenny!

JENNY L   Oh, I'd like it very much, Mrs Hedley. It's the
only thing that keeps me going when that
Lizzie gets at me in the kitchen – thinking of
yer cakes and scones.   40

*She takes the parcels and puts her coat on. Tom
puts on a jacket. They move and sit to wait for the
cart. Mrs Hedley exits.*

Scene 8

October, 1914

*Jenny Lucas and Tom are waiting for Jenny's lift
home a little way outside Tom's cottage.*

TOM   Is that the only thought that keeps you going –
me mam's teas?

JENNY L   Don't be silly!

TOM   Well then, what?

JENNY L   What do you mean, what?   5

TOM   I do like seeing you, Jenny Lucas.

JENNY L   Me too – seeing you I mean – I see enough of me!

TOM   So – we're **walking out**, as they say?

JENNY L   I'd like to walk out with you, Tom Hedley.

TOM   Would you really?   10

JENNY L   Really I would. *(Tom takes her hand)* Tom …

TOM   What?

JENNY L   Has yer mam never wanted to get married
again? Like me dad did?

TOM	I don't know – I've never thought about it. I think she's a bit lonely, mind. Poor mam!	15
JENNY L	We'll have to matchmake for her – then there'll be someone else she can cook for.	
TOM	She's always at it! She's going to send stuff off to Master Will – we got a letter from him at the training camp last week. The food's dreadful! It was great to hear from him – I'm glad he remembered us.	20
JENNY L	Bet he's homesick! Like you said – I can't see him being a soldier. He doesn't know a bee from a bull's foot! Not like Mattie, or that other lad he goes about with – John Watson. They're the right sort to be soldiers, I reckon. But Hannah told Mattie she'd thump him if he joined up, now she's … *(she stops herself just in time)*	25 30
TOM	I know – expecting! Mattie did tell me.	
JENNY L	You're his pal – you have words with him. It's not fair on Hannah, and it won't be fair on the bairn when it's born.	
TOM	Mebbes – it's a hard one that.	35
JENNY L	Well, would you join up, if you were Mattie?	
TOM	If I was nineteen and old enough to join up, you mean?	
JENNY L	No – if you had a wife and … and …	
TOM	And a baby on the way?	40
JENNY L	That and all.	
TOM	What difference would it make?	
JENNY L	What difference? Tom Hedley! Of course it would make a difference! Why put yerself in	

so much danger when you don't have to   45
and when you've got people to look after …
People needing you.

TOM   Yes, I know. That's exactly why I *would* join up.
To defend them from the Germans.

JENNY L But all that's happening in France, Tom.   50
It's not as real as what's happening here.
What if Hannah got sick when she was
having the baby?

TOM   All right then – you say it's not as real. *(pause)*
Britain's an island, isn't it? King George V   55
lives in London, doesn't he?

JENNY L Yes! So?

TOM   Have you ever been all the way round the
coast? Have you ever seen the King or been
to London? *(she shakes her head)* But you   60
know those things are true and real.

JENNY L Like saying yer prayers even though you've
never seen God?

TOM   Now that's something I'm not too sure about,
not after me dad getting killed in the pit.   65
But think a bit! You haven't said Mattie
shouldn't be working down the mine, and
that's dangerous!

JENNY L But he doesn't have any choice – it's his job.
Anyway, I'm not sure as we should be   70
fighting the Germans in France. Just because
that **Archduke** person got shot.

TOM   *(pause)* All right. You're always going on about
Lizzie in the kitchen and how she doesn't
care about hurting people, and how   75
greedy she is …

JENNY L   … always wanting to be more important than anyone else …

TOM   Yes! So, the **Hun's** like that. Only much grander, of course. Just waiting for an 80 excuse to steal other people's countries and marching all over Belgium even though Belgium was supposed to be safe. The newspapers said we were *bound in honour* to stand up to the Hun – show him we 85 wouldn't tolerate bullies. I mean, Britain's got a great Empire – that's why it's called 'Great' Britain! We can't show ourselves up.

JENNY L   It all sounds very clever, everything you've said. But I bet most of the ordinary German 90 soldiers would much rather be home with their wives and sweethearts and families. Anyway, Tom Hedley, you talk about making a stand – and you're going on about Lizzie. If you ask me, it'll be half Lizzie's fault if 95 Mattie joins up. She and that nasty Polly Jackson keep going on about a poster they saw in Lakely. The one that says you should tell yer *best boy* he's got to go to war.

TOM   But he's not her *best boy*! 100

JENNY L   Yes, but Hannah says she always wanted him to be. She wanted him to court her before he got his eye on Hannah *(Dr Lindsay appears)* … Oh look, Tom … There's Dr Lindsay! I'll have to go. See you soon. 105

TOM   Bye, Jenny! *(he pecks her on the cheek)*

JENNY L   No hanky panky, yer mam said!

TOM   It'll keep! *(Jenny exits)*

Scene 9

October, 1914

Tom is looking off into the distance. Mattie enters.

TOM   *(turns round)* What are you doing here?

MATTIE   Fancied a bit of a walk, that's all. Finished yer courting, have you?

TOM   Watch it!

MATTIE   *(sits down)* Aye, it's a grand night! *(rummages 5 around on the ground)* How's that for a prize conker!

TOM   Bit **long in the tooth** for the Conker Championship, aren't you?

MATTIE   Hannah said the first time she fancied me 10 was when she saw me beat Joe Robson into second place!

TOM   I'll believe you!

They sit in silence for a while. Mattie throws his conker from hand to hand, then places it down and lies back, hands behind his head.

MATTIE   Ah, that's good. No **jabbering on** up here.

TOM   No need – you and me. 15

MATTIE   Aye, brains and brawn! You're the brains of course.

TOM   I didn't show much brain when I fell off the wall onto yer dad's prize cabbages. You didn't waste words then, either. 20

MATTIE   I'd spent all me spare time watering the damn things! Dad went nuts!

TOM   Never **snitched** on me, did you?

MATTIE   Reckon I should have done.

TOM   Maybe you would have if the alarm hadn't   25
rung from the pithead.

MATTIE   Aye. That was a sad day. *(silence)*

TOM   Never forgotten that. Me dad being fetched up
by your dad, and you trying to help.

MATTIE   Luck of the draw – *my* dad could have been   30
on that shift easy enough.

*Silence. Mattie sits up, stands up, walks around
scuffing the ground, then sits down again, his back
to Tom.*

TOM   What's up, then?

MATTIE   Nowt. *(another silence)* Have you heard any
more from Master Will?

TOM   Not really. Last letter just said something   35
about going where there was tunnelling to
do. Said they were recruiting miners as well,
and that the commanding officers got
excited when they heard Will's dad owned a
mine. Thought Will would be a bit of an   40
expert.

MATTIE   They'll be in for a disappointment, then. Never
met such a **cack-handed** bloke.

TOM   Wouldn't even trust him with a gardening fork!

MATTIE   *(laughs)* Aye! He's nice enough, mind. Not   45
stuck up. *(thoughtfully)* A bit weird. Got his
head in the clouds. Like you sometimes.

*Tom pushes him over and they have a brief
wrestling match. Mattie breaks away suddenly.*

MATTIE	Should be settled now, but … I just don't know where to put the next foot anymore! Looking forward to the bairn coming, though. 50 And, mind, I do love Hannah … It's just this war. And the work at the pit down to four days a week.
TOM	I thought his Lordship was giving you and the other lads work on the estate to make up 55 the money?
MATTIE	Aye, he's a fair man. It feels like charity, though. I want to do something really worthwhile. I want to know where I'm heading.
TOM	Where do you think you *are* heading? 60
MATTIE	France, mebbes.
TOM	Enlisting?
MATTIE	I'm thinking … *(he gets up and throws the conkers at Tom)* Here, take them …

Mattie exits. Tom looks after him, then exits in the other direction.

Scene 10

The present day

Enter Jenny Clark and Mrs Clark. Jenny takes a small white feather from the trunk and shows it to Mrs Clark.

JENNY C	What's this, mum?
MRS CLARK	I can't imagine why anyone should want to keep that. If it's what I think it's for, that is.
JENNY C	What's that?

MRS CLARK   Women used to hand them out to young   5
             men in wartime – to shame them into
             joining the army. Trying to make out they
             were cowards … you know.

             Exit Jenny Clark and Mrs Clark.

Scene 11

February, 1915

*Hannah, Mattie and Jenny Lucas are in Byford
Church listening to the Vicar. Also in the
congregation are Polly and Lizzie (with Tom, Mrs
Hedley and other villagers if desired).*

VICAR   We have in mind today those brave soldiers
         who have volunteered to help our French
         allies against the common enemy. In the
         words of the War Secretary, Lord Kitchener,
         it will be their duty to set an example of   5
         discipline and perfect steadiness under fire.
         Our thoughts and prayers go with them.

ALL   *(they sing a hymn)* 'I vow to thee, my country, all
         earthly things above,
         Entire and whole and perfect, the service   10
         of my love:
         The love that asks no question, the love that
         stands the test,
         That lays upon the altar the dearest and
         the best;   15
         The love that never falters, the love that pays
         the price,
         The love that makes undaunted the final
         sacrifice.'

VICAR   I would like to draw the attention of the   20
congregation to the fact that the recruiting
station in Lakely will be open every day this
week from ten in the morning until three in
the afternoon. If any young man in the
congregation should wish to do his duty   25
by his country, here is his opportunity. There
may be no others!

Vicar exits. The congregation prepare to leave.
They whisper amongst themselves. Lizzie and
Polly nudge each other and giggle. They follow
Mattie, Hannah and Jenny. Polly holds a white
feather behind her back.

LIZZIE   *(calling)* Mattie Clark!

MATTIE   Now what does she want?

HANNAH   Ignore her!   30

LIZZIE   Mattie Clark!

POLLY   Mattie Clark! Best boy!

LIZZIE   *(giggling)* Shh!

MATTIE   What d'you want, then, Lizzie Palmer?

LIZZIE   Isn't it time you joined up, Mattie Clark?   35
(with exaggerated importance) Your country
needs you!

HANNAH   The cheek of it! Get on yer way, both of you –
go on!

MATTIE   Don't take on, Hannah. I'll sort them out   40
meself.

POLLY   With this, Mattie? *(she hands him the white feather)*

MATTIE   Ugh! *(makes an exclamation of disgust)*

JENNY L You don't know what you're talking about!
(picks up the feather and hands it back to Lizzie)
If you're so brave why don't you go and be   45
nurses and wipe up all the blood!

HANNAH My Mattie's as brave as any! Just the other day
he stayed with John Watson down the pit
when a prop collapsed, and John got his leg
hurt. He had to wait hours for help, and   50
the whole section could have come down on
the both of them.

LIZZIE Says you!

MATTIE Now listen here. I'll not be made a fool of by
two lasses that haven't the sense they   55
were born with. I've made up me mind
already what I'm doing without anyone else's
help. Now get away home with you. Oh, and
Jenny's right – take the beastly thing
yerselves, unless you've got the guts to   60
join up. And next time you've a job to be
done, you do it, Lizzie Palmer – don't be
getting Polly to do yer dirty work. Thank
God I saw through you in time!

*Mattie thrusts the feather into Lizzie's hand. Lizzie
and Polly look rather abashed, but cover it up by
sniggering. Polly and Lizzie exit, as do any other
remaining members of the congregation.*

HANNAH *(very quietly)* You've made up yer mind,   65
Mattie?

MATTIE I know you won't like it, lass, but I'm off to
Lakely in the morning. There's a whole
crowd of us going to enlist together. If
there's tunnelling work to be done in   70

France they'll need us miners. Lord Fordham
says he'll give all the families back here good
money. He'll look after you all, I know he
will. And look, Hannah. What we'll be doing
– it's not much different to here – not more   75
dangerous, I mean. We'll be underground!

HANNAH   But the baby, Mattie!

MATTIE   I'll get leave! And the war'll be over soon. It's
bound to be.

HANNAH   Oh Mattie! *(she runs to him and hugs him close.*   80
He is embarrassed)

MATTIE   Got to get a good night's sleep! *(he goes)*

Hannah turns in tears to Jenny.

HANNAH   Don't you leave me!

Scene 12

February, 1915

*At the station. Sound of steam train. Mattie enters,
putting his cap on after leaving the train. Tom
enters after alighting from further up the train.*

TOM   There you are!

MATTIE   I don't need you to see me off to France yet,
you know. Who knows, they mightn't even
want me!

TOM   I'm coming too!   5

MATTIE   And I know me own way up the street!

TOM   I mean, I'm coming to join up.

MATTIE   Are you mad? You've got to be nineteen to
enlist! You're only – what is it – sixteen?

TOM	Seventeen in June. And I'm brighter than	10
	Ned Watkins, even though he's twenty-two!	
	And just as strong.	

MATTIE   True enough, but … I mean …

TOM   Well … Come on then …

MATTIE   They'll turn you away.   15

TOM   I'll just say I'm nineteen next week – then it
won't seem so bad. It's worth a try, anyway!
Come on then!

MATTIE   *(shaking his head)* Well, I don't know … !

*They turn to go together. Jenny Lucas enters,
running. She has also been on the train.*

JENNY L   Tom! Wait!   20

TOM   Jenny? Why aren't you back at the Hall?

JENNY L   I begged them to let me swap me half day.
I know what you're up to and you musn't!

TOM   You can't stop me.

JENNY L   I just can't bear it!   25

TOM   *(he comes over to her)* Please, Jenny. *(he takes her
hand)*

JENNY L   What about yer place at grammar school?

TOM   The books will still be there when I get back.
(his face softens) Look, I'm a bit scared too.
And I need you to look after Mam when   30
I'm out there. Will you do that? *(he turns away
to Mattie)* Please, Jenny!

*Jenny sighs and watches Tom and Mattie walk
away.*

Scene 13

February, 1915

The Recruiting Officer and Dr Lindsay are sitting behind two folding tables in the recruiting office. Mattie and Tom enter. There are some men from the village bustling about.

MATTIE	*(looking around, whispering)* Half the county's here!
RECRUITING OFFICER	Next! *(Mattie steps forward)* Name?
MATTIE	Matthew John Clark.
RECRUITING OFFICER	Age?
MATTIE	Nineteen years, eleven months.
RECRUITING OFFICER	Occupation?
MATTIE	Miner.
RECRUITING OFFICER	Married?
MATTIE	Yes.
RECRUITING OFFICER	Have you ever served in the armed forces before?
MATTIE	No.
RECRUITING OFFICER	Right, lad. We'll check your height and chest measurement – let the doctor look you over.

Mattie moves over to Dr Lindsay who proceeds to make the checks.

RECRUITING OFFICER	Next! *(Tom approaches the Recruiting Officer)* Name?
TOM	Thomas Edward Hedley.
RECRUITING OFFICER	Age?
TOM	*(swallows hard)* I'll be nineteen next Sunday, Sir!
RECRUITING OFFICER	Occupation?

5

10

15

20

27

TOM	Miner.
RECRUITING OFFICER	Married?
TOM	No.
RECRUITING OFFICER	Well then, lad, it's just as well. You'd be telling her a pack of lies too!

25

TOM	Sir?
RECRUITING OFFICER	*(tiredly)* Have you ever served in the armed forces before?
TOM	No.
RECRUITING OFFICER	I bet you haven't! Oh, go on with you. See the doctor. *(Tom moves to the doctor as Mattie stands to one side)*

30

DR LINDSAY	Let's see now. Tom Hedley, isn't it. *(checks his height)* My, you've grown! *(checks his chest measurement)* Well, that seems fine. *(holds down Tom's tongue)* Say 'ah'.

35

TOM	Agh!
DR LINDSAY	You're a credit to your dad! And just as foolhardy too. Now then, can you read that sign over there?
TOM	2nd Battalion, Lakely Division.

40

DR LINDSAY	That all seems very satisfactory. I can't say as I'd wish it that way, but there you are …
RECRUITING OFFICER	We've a lot to get through. Just read this card together, lads.
TOM AND MATTIE	I … swear by Almighty God that I will be faithful and bear true allegiance to His Majesty King George V, his heirs and successors, and that I will as in duty bound, honestly and faithfully defend His Majesty,

45

His Heirs and successors, in Person, Crown   50
and Dignity against all enemies, according to
the conditions of my service.

RECRUITING OFFICER   Sign here please.

Tom and Mattie sign a piece of paper.

RECRUITING OFFICER   Over here, lads. I'll get you your money and
the rest of your orders.   55

Tom and Mattie exit with the Recruiting Officer.

Scene 14

February, 1915

Outside the recruiting office. Dr Lindsay closes his bag and moves over to where Jenny Lucas is sitting.

DR LINDSAY   Jenny from the Hall isn't it?

JENNY L   Ye … yes, Sir.

DR LINDSAY   Are you all right?

JENNY L   I'll be as right as rain in a minute, Sir.

DR LINDSAY   Would my handkerchief help?   5

JENNY L   Thank you, Sir.

DR LINDSAY   Would this have something to do with young
Tom?

JENNY L   How did you know?

DR LINDSAY   I've just given him his medical.   10

JENNY L   Please say he didn't pass, Sir!

DR LINDSAY   I had to pass him A1. Reluctantly, I may add.

JENNY L   Oh! *(she blows her nose again)* What's A1, Sir?

DR LINDSAY	Means he's a fine upstanding lad. Right height, chest measurement and so on. It's my opinion he ought to be thinking twice about throwing himself away in France! 15
JENNY L	It's not throwing himself away!
DR LINDSAY	Forgive me. I shouldn't have said that. It was tactless. Oh, the idealism of youth! 20
JENNY L	*(looking confused)* I beg yer pardon, Sir?
DR LINDSAY	Nothing, lass. Miss Jenny, I should say. You're a good girl. I've watched you and young Tom. Would I be right to say you're walking out together? 25
JENNY L	Something like that, Sir. I know it's not been much time, but we really do like each other. Hannah – that's me sister – says we're too young, but I was sixteen just after Christmas and he'll be seventeen in three months time – oh, oh … 30
DR LINDSAY	You wish you hadn't told me he was only sixteen, don't you?
JENNY L	*(whispers)* Yes, Sir.
DR LINDSAY	Do you think I didn't guess? 35
JENNY L	Please – can't you go back in and tell them he's too young? I know he wants to go and fight and I'm so proud of him, but I just don't think I can bear him being gone and I don't really know what the war has to do with us even though he's tried to explain over and over again! 40
DR LINDSAY	Not my job to tell them anything, I'm afraid. And he's **taken the King's shilling** – it really

is too late. All over England, there's decent,   45
brave lads like Tom signing up. Recruiting
officers telling them to go round the block
and come back in half an hour when they're
nineteen and old enough. Why, I measured a
lad last week that was too small, and the   50
sergeant just fetched a box for him to stand
on – told me I needed new spectacles and
said to measure him again! Ah – here comes
your young man. Well I'll be off. And look,
Miss Jenny, you just call on me if things get   55
difficult. Come and have a chat if you want.
I can do that at least.

Dr Lindsay leaves. Mattie and Tom enter.

TOM   I'm all fixed up, Jenny! Shall we get off back
then? I'm not looking forward to telling
Mam! Have to get it over with, though!   60
Don't suppose you'd break the news for me?

*Sounds of the train again as Jenny Lucas, Mattie and
Tom exit. Dr Lindsay looks after them, thoughtfully
and then exits in the opposite direction.*

Scene 15

February, 1915

*Outside Mrs Hedley's cottage. Jenny Lucas enters,
running.*

JENNY L   *(breathlessly)* Mrs Hedley! Mrs Hedley!

MRS HEDLEY   What is it, Jenny? Have you seen Tom? He's
been missing all day!

JENNY L   I don't know how to tell you.

MRS HEDLEY	Is he hurt?	5
JENNY L	No …	
MRS HEDLEY	Well what then?	
JENNY L	He wanted me to tell you …	
MRS HEDLEY	What's he been up to? What's going on? *(silence)* For heaven's sake, Jenny, just tell me!	10
JENNY L	He's enlisted!	
MRS HEDLEY	He's enlisted? But he's only sixteen! And what about his scholarship?	
JENNY L	I've tried and tried to persuade him not to go. But they're taking all sorts of lads – some of them not even all there, if you know what I mean. And lads not tall enough or big enough. If there's someone not old enough, they just tell him to come back when he is, like in an hour's time. It's mad!	15 20
MRS HEDLEY	Oh God! *(she sits on a chair suddenly)* I don't know how I'll bear it! First his dad, then him!	
JENNY L	*(she kneels beside Mrs Hedley and puts her arm around her)* Not all the soldiers die, surely?	
MRS HEDLEY	Why didn't he tell me he was going to join up himself?	25
JENNY L	He was too frightened.	
MRS HEDLEY	That's a fine thing! Off to fight the Hun and he's frightened of his mam! And did he think I'd cut off me nose to spite me own face? Nothing I can say or do will make any earthly difference, so I may as well show him I love him while he's still here and not be shouting at him. He *is* coming back home	30

isn't he? Before he goes off to the army,
I mean? Oh, please tell me he is!   35

JENNY L   They've given him a railway warrant to get to
where he's got to be trained – but he has to
wait here till Monday, so he'll be home a few
days yet.

Tom enters.

TOM   *(rather sheepishly)* Mam?   40

MRS HEDLEY   Tom! How could you! Oh, Tom … *(she runs to
him and hugs him)* I'm proud of you, lad, really
I am. Though I'm cross enough to burst.
Such a stupid war! I wish there was another
way for you to go on but I know there isn't.   45
And I know it's no good arguing – yer dad
would have done just the same. Now … *(she
blows her nose)* … Let's get some clean socks
and treacle toffees packed first. What else …
Oh dear, I don't know! Never mind, it's a   50
few days yet till Monday. Will you be seeing
Master Will when you're away?

TOM   Probably in the same battalion. Mattie and most
of the other lads from the pit joined up.
I think we'll all be together. I'll stick with   55
Mattie, Mam. I'll keep an eye on him for
Hannah, eh, Jenny? He'll have to show me
how to go about tunnelling and such.

MRS HEDLEY   Well, you'll all need lots of sweets then.

TOM   That's my mam! Look after her for me,   60
Jenny?

Jenny, too tearful to reply, nods her head.

TOM	You'll come up for yer tea on Sundays, just like as if I was here?
JENNY L	*(fiercely)* If you think I'm staying in the kitchen in the Hall with that Lizzie and Polly any 65 more than I have to … Oh, I could kill them!
TOM	I promise you one thing – nothing those two said made a bit of difference to Mattie and me.
MRS HEDLEY	Well, then, let's have a really good tea before Jenny has to go back. 70

Mrs Hedley, Tom and Jenny Lucas move to the back of the stage.

Scene 16

The present day

Enter Jenny Clark. She takes a piece of paper from the trunk. Mrs Hedley, Jenny Lucas and Tom speak as voices from the past.

MRS HEDLEY	Susannah Hedley, widow of Edward Hedley …
TOM	Tom Hedley, soldier, son of Susannah Hedley – sweetheart of Jenny Lucas …
JENNY L	Jenny Lucas, kitchen maid of Byford Hall …
JENNY C	*(reading from the paper)* 'We, the above, 5 promise to keep each other in our hearts through this difficult time, wherever we may be. And we promise to meet – all three together – in happier times ahead. Signed by all of us: 10th February, 1915.' 10

Exit all characters.

Act Two

Scene 1

The present day

Enter Jenny Clark. She is reading from a small book which she has taken from the trunk used in Act One.

JENNY C   '10th April, 1915. My name is Jenny Lucas and I am sixteen years old. My sweetheart is Tom Hedley. His dad was killed in the pit and he lives with his mam in one of the houses up the hill. Lord Fordham owns the pit – I work 5 for him at the big house. He's been very good to Tom's mam since Tom went away to fight. He pays the rent for her sweet shop. He's been good to all the mining families from round here.' 10

Exit Jenny Clark.

Scene 2

April, 1915

Outside Byford Hall. Jenny Lucas is sitting cross-legged, reading what she has just written in her diary.

JENNY L   'I miss Tom very much and that's why I thought I'd keep this diary, to help fill in the time. I want to be able to tell him and Mattie, my sister Hannah's husband – he's away fighting too – I want to tell them all about Hannah's 5 new baby when it's born – when it gets its first tooth and things. Mattie and Tom have been training – now we're waiting to hear

when they're off to France. We all keep
hoping the war will be over soon, but   10
Dr Lindsay, who knows a lot, says maybe it
won't.'

Enter Polly and Lizzie.

POLLY   Writing to yer best boy, Jenny Lucas?

LIZZIE   We could tell him a thing or two, couldn't we!

POLLY   We've seen you, haven't we!   15

LIZZIE   Oh yes we have. We know what you get up to
           on yer days off.

JENNY L   I don't know what you're talking about.

LIZZIE   Little Miss Innocent, isn't she.

POLLY   Butter wouldn't melt in her mouth …   20

LIZZIE   I think I'll write to that Tom Hedley of hers …

POLLY   If he's not shot to bits already …

LIZZIE   Or got himself a **blighty one** so as he can get
           home for the Christmas party …

POLLY   Or run off with a mademoiselle.   25

LIZZIE   That'd be likely. He hasn't got what it takes. You
           know that, don't you, Polly. Remember that
           time down by the river?

POLLY   Yes, Lizzie. *(collapses in giggles)*

LIZZIE   You didn't half try hard. I saw you. I could   30
           swear on the Bible!

JENNY L   Shut up, you lying, horrible, mean thing!

POLLY   *(giggles)* Shall I tell you what he did? *(she
           whispers in Lizzie's ear)*

LIZZIE   Oooh – we'd better not tell little Miss Lucas.
           She might be shocked!   35

JENNY L   All right then, clever! First you're telling me he
          hasn't got it in him, and now you're telling
          me he's been up to no good! I think you've
          forgotten who you're talking about. And
          that's hardly surprising – you go with so   40
          many, don't you, Polly Watkins! *(she sticks her
          tongue out at Polly)*

LIZZIE   Oooh – temper, temper. Let's see what Miss
          Firebrand is writing to her dearly beloved.
          (she snatches at the diary)

JENNY L   *(snatches it back and runs away)* You get off that.
          You're not fit to be in the same room as   45
          them – Mattie and Tom. Go and find some
          real cowards to walk out with – you'll be well
          matched! *(she goes)*

LIZZIE   *(in a loud voice)* Come on then, Polly. We'll tell
          Cook how prim and proper little Miss   50
          Lucas spends the time when she should be
          working.

          Lizzie and Polly run off giggling.

Scene 3
April, 1915

*Outside the Hedleys' cottage. Mrs Hedley enters,
reading a postcard. Jenny Lucas runs in with a letter.*

JENNY L   Mrs Hedley! Mrs Hedley! There's a letter from
              Tom!

MRS HEDLEY   And I've got a postcard!

JENNY L   Just a postcard?

MRS HEDLEY   That's all right now! Mothers have to get to   5
              know their place! It says 'Fit and well. Have

plenty of socks and treacle toffees, but some sugar, tea and candles would come in handy. Don't worry. Will write again soon.'

JENNY L   Shall I read you me letter?   10

MRS HEDLEY   No, lass – that's between you and him.

JENNY L   I won't read the private bits … 'We've had a good time at the training camp – all us lads from Byford together …'

MRS HEDLEY   I'm glad he hasn't been lonely!   15

JENNY L   '… it's been really hard work, though. Freezing cold water for washing …'

MRS HEDLEY   The poor souls!

JENNY L   '… lots of running about, and learning to march. I might be quite a good dancer but   20 I'm rotten at marching! I'm not too sure how I feel about using the bayonet – even less about using it on a real person. But whenever things get tough I try to remember my dad. I know he would have enlisted straight   25 away, and I know he would have thought it a privilege to fight for his country. We're being posted this week. I promise I'll write as soon as I possibly can when we get settled. Mattie and I hope we'll see Will. There's a good   30 chance we'll be joining his battalion, maybe even his company …' *(she skims over the next bit)* … This is for me …

MRS HEDLEY   That's all right lass. I'll go and put the kettle on …

Jenny sits down to read the private bit of her letter.

Scene 4

The present day

In her kitchen, Jenny Clark unfolds Tom's love letter and reads aloud into her mobile phone.

JENNY C   Listen to this, Sarah – it's a love letter and it's
really romantic! 'I hope you know how much
I miss you. I would have liked to walk the
lanes with you now the spring has come. But
I really mean what I say about fighting for   5
my country being a privilege – I just had to
give myself that chance. Will you keep writing
to me and letting me know if Mam is well?
I look forward to your letters every day, and if
I'm expecting one and it doesn't come,   10
my heart sinks – then I think perhaps you've
found someone else to walk out with! But when
your letters *do* come I just know you care about
me, and that helps to get me through.'

Scene 5

April, 1915

In a bunker in France. The Corporal enters with Mattie and Tom who are carrying their kit.

CORPORAL   Right, lads. Here you are. Not much room with
twenty of you in here but it'll soon feel like
home! Make sure you don't bump your heads
on the bunk above! **Grub**'s up soon, when
the others get back, then kip – that's sleep   5
to you! I'll be wanting you up and ready for
action in the morning. **Shoring up**, that's
what we're on at the moment.

TOM AND MATTIE	Yes, Sir!
CORPORAL	Understand you knew Second Lieutenant 10 Fordham back home?
TOM AND MATTIE	Yes, Sir.
MATTIE	Knew, Sir?
TOM	Is he all right, Sir?
CORPORAL	Just a manner of speaking! Yes, he's all right. 15 Be over to see you, like enough. Just remember, he's 'Sir' to you, whatever you all got up to back home. Well, nightie night!
TOM	*(not sure how to respond)* Er, yes, Sir. Nightie … er … goodnight, Sir. 20

Corporal exits just as Will enters.

CORPORAL	New lads, Sir. Think you know them! *(exit Corporal)*
WILL	Mattie! *(looks delighted)*
MATTIE	Watcha, Master Will!
WILL	This is never … Tom! You're a sly one, Tom Hedley! Well I'll be damned! Oh, this is 25 splendid! What's it like back home? Have you just got here? How was the crossing? Are you the only ones from Byford?
TOM	There's Harry and Jack at least.
MATTIE	They're **billeted** next door. 30
TOM	What's it like here, Master Will, I mean, Sir?
WILL	Oh, not bad at all! Not like it is at the Front, anyway. My God, I'll be glad of you, Mattie Clark. I'm sick to death of pretending I know what I'm talking about when it comes to 35 tunnelling.

MATTIE   So what's to be done?

WILL   So far it's mostly been keeping things safe
underground. It's taken months to tunnel
along, yard by yard, and place all the   40
explosives, so the dampness gets at the
insulation – we've got to be testing them all
the time. Then we've got to watch out for gas
– there's **canaries** carried in, just like in the
mines back home.   45

TOM   *(eagerly)* What about the enemy? Do you see
much of them?

WILL   You can hear the German sentries blazing away
when they think we're up to something big.
But so far I don't think it's like being in the   50
front line. Not that I'm sorry.

MATTIE   We chatted to three lads coming back out on
leave. They'd been at the Front.

TOM   One of them said a funny thing. Said how if you
were out on patrol by yerself, you quite   55
enjoyed it all.

MATTIE   Yes, but if you were waiting for one of yer
group to come back you'd be worried the
whole time.

TOM   Hey, is it true what they say about the lice?   60

WILL   *(laughs)* In the frosts, we used to hang our
shirts up outside to freeze the little beasts.
Then we'd brush them off before the sun
rose – before they came to life again. Roll on
winter again! I tell you, if a man had the   65
craftiness of a woman and the cunning of a
louse he could conquer the world. That's

going to be the first line of the book I'll write when all this is over.

TOM *(laughs)* What about the food? 70

WILL Make sure you get them to send you out sugar, tea, **condensed milk**, candles … If you've got that and some bread, you're a millionaire. I tell you, by the time you've been here a few weeks you'll be able to tell whether the 75 water's been stored in a BP tin or a Shell tin. And you'll never want to see corned beef again. Well, lads, I'd better go off and pretend to take charge of something. *(turning to go)* Of course, you know the drill 80 – I'm 'Sir' to you when anyone else is listening.

TOM AND MATTIE Yes, Sir! *(they salute)*

WILL *(turning back impulsively)* Hey – I can't tell you how good it is to see you lads. I sometimes don't think I can … I mean … oh, damn! 85 *(he almost runs off)*

MATTIE *(looks after him)* Not a good start, would you say?

Scene 6

May, 1915

Outside the Hedleys' cottage. Jenny Lucas and Mrs Hedley are folding sheets or doing some other household job.

JENNY L I wonder if Tom will be able to bring us back some presents from France? Do you think he'll be home for Christmas?

MRS HEDLEY That's a long way off yet. But he'll be due some leave by then, surely. 5

JENNY L	It'll be our Hannah's first Christmas with the baby, so Mattie will want to be there.
MRS HEDLEY	Now when's that baby due?
JENNY L	Any day now.

Scene 7

May, 1915

In the bunker. Tom and Mattie are polishing their uniform belts.

TOM   Hill 60 – Lovers' Knoll.

MATTIE   Yer what?

TOM   When they dug out the railway cutting here
fifty years ago – that's when the hill got
made, from all the earth piled up alongside.   5
And then the courting couples came. That's
what they started to call it – Côte des
Amants – Lovers' Knoll.

MATTIE   *(sarcastically)* That'd be right. I'll remember it
when I'm flat on me stomach, face to face   10
with a **Jerry** and his bayonet. Why're you
thinking of that, **any road?**

TOM   I'm going to tell Jenny when I write. Then she
can think of us with our arms round each
other instead of me shuffling along on me   15
belly waiting to be blown to pieces. I don't
half miss her, Mattie. Hope she hasn't found
another lad to walk out with.

MATTIE   She might if she finds out about the lice in yer
tunic! *(Tom makes to hit him)* No, shouldn't   20
think so. Not if she's like my Hannah. Stick

	to you like glue she will! Hey, Tom, the bairn's probably born by now!	
TOM	What are you hoping for?	
MATTIE	A boy, I think. We'll need a few more men in the country when all this is over.	25

Will enters – they stand to attention.

WILL	Lads!	
TOM AND MATTIE	Sir!	
WILL	Time to get a move on.	
TOM AND MATTIE	Yes Sir!	30
WILL	Right – now then. Tunnel five's finished. 'C' Section's going in to lay explosives. Private Hedley, Private Clark – I've been asked to send two lads up to the listening post. That's you two. Take the gear with you. And remember – we need to know exactly where the enemy are underground without them knowing either where you are, or where the explosives are.	35
TOM AND MATTIE	Yes, Lieutenant Fordham.	40
WILL	Any unusual noise, or any sudden silence from the enemy – one of you gets straight back along and gives me or Captain Knox the warning. We can't use the field phone – the lines have been cut. Now, there's a real danger the enemy could collapse the mine before we finish packing the explosives. They've just got to toss in a grenade and … Right? I'll be along to see you soon.	45
TOM AND MATTIE	Right, Sir.	50

WILL   We're going to **lay the charge** at 0600 hours. Good luck!

TOM AND MATTIE   Thanks, Sir. *(Will goes)*

TOM   Seems to me this Hill 60 of ours gets passed from one side to the other like a cake at a   55 party.

MATTIE   Why do we need it, any road?

TOM   Jerry wants to get a good view of **Wipers** from the top – so *we* keep trying to blow it up. Then he tries blowing up a few of *our*   60 tunnels – just to keep the score even!

MATTIE   Righto – are we on then?

TOM   We're on – well, under!

Tom and Mattie take their equipment and crawl along to the listening post, Mattie ahead of Tom.

Scene 8

May, 1915

In the listening post, a short offshoot of the main tunnel where 'C' Section is laying explosives. There is the sound of scraping from the German tunnel only two or three feet away from them, under the hillside. Tom and Mattie whisper to each other.

MATTIE   They're *this* near!

TOM   Just stay there, Jerry.

Will is standing at the end of the tunnel. He is very nervous.

WILL   *(to himself)* Right, Will Fordham. Second Lieutenant Fordham. Will Fordham of

Byford Hall, Lakely, Great Britain. When   5
the war is over – back to Cambridge. Read
History. Just think – I'll be *part of* history!
Plenty of soldiers before me – not afraid.
Brave men. Just got to get on and do it …
Right … The tunnel. Just like a fox –   10
hounds baying at it. No, no – *I* am master of
my fate – it matters not how strait the gate –
how black the night … Oh God! *(he crouches
down and crawls towards Mattie and Tom, who
are listening with their instruments against the
wall of the listening post)*

WILL   Lads?

TOM   All right, Sir.   15

MATTIE   Sh! Listen! *(the scraping has stopped)*

WILL   What? *(he crawls past Tom and behind Mattie to hear)*

MATTIE   Jerry's stopped.

TOM   I'll report back … *(he starts to turn round)*

WILL   NO!   20

TOM   Sir … ?

WILL   Jerry'll hear you – and the whole section's in
here. Use the phone …

MATTIE   Line's cut, Sir. You told us!

TOM   I've got to warn the others, Sir.   25

WILL   NO!!

MATTIE   Get him out of here!

WILL   Rat in a trap – fox in a trap … *(he is babbling
this over and over again)*

MATTIE   Belt him, Tom – shut him up!

TOM	Sorry, Will – Sir! *(Tom knocks Will unconscious)*	30

MATTIE Now go – GO! *(Tom drags Will back outside. He stands)*

TOM *(shouting)* Captain Knox! Captain Kno …

There is a huge explosion. Tom is knocked to the ground alongside Will.

Scene 9

May, 1915

The characters are in position from the previous scene: Mattie is motionless, Tom and Will are lying crumpled up together. Captain Knox enters.

WILL God, my head! Someone – someone hit me! Tom Hedley? What did you do that for? God, it hurts – my leg!

CAPTAIN KNOX Are you all right? Are you all right?

WILL Tom Hedley! Private Hedley! Speak to me! 5 Not dead are you? You're not dead, are you! Tom – why did you hit me?

CAPTAIN KNOX He hit you?

WILL I think so! Oh God, my leg!

CAPTAIN KNOX Soon have you sorted. As for this one … 10 *(to Tom)* Get up now! Stop shamming!

TOM *(groggily)* Mattie, did you get out? Mattie? Sir – Captain Knox, Sir … did he get out? Will, did I hurt you?

CAPTAIN KNOX Right, I've heard enough! On your feet, 15 Private Hedley!

TOM	Sir? I don't know what …
CAPTAIN KNOX	You hit this officer here?
TOM	Well yes, Sir … I … I …
CAPTAIN KNOX	You're under arrest!

20

Scene 10

June, 1915

At an army barracks, about three weeks later. Captain Knox pulls Tom to his feet. Major Henderson, Mr Hines the Orderly and an NCO enter. The NCO comes forward to take charge of Tom. Captain Knox withdraws to stand beside the Orderly, and the Major takes command, reading the charge.

MAJOR Private Thomas Edward Hedley, the charge against you is that on the 20th May, 1915, you did wilfully strike a superior officer with the express purpose of deserting your post, thereby creating a disturbance which   5
betrayed the position of 'C' Company to the enemy. This resulted in an explosion in which all members of the said company perished, with the exception of Second Lieutenant William Fordham, the superior   10
officer in question, and yourself. What do you plead?

TOM I … *(he is confused)*

MAJOR Private Thomas Edward Hedley, did you strike Second Lieutenant Fordham?   15

TOM Yes, Sir, I …

MAJOR I would like to call upon Captain Rupert Knox. *(Captain Knox steps forward)* Captain Knox, did

you see the defendant, Private Thomas
Hedley, strike Lieutenant William Fordham?   20

CAPTAIN KNOX   After the explosion, I found the two men,
Private Hedley and Second Lieutenant
Fordham, lying on the ground. Private
Hedley appeared to be unconscious although
I was not able to establish whether he was   25
in fact only pretending to be injured.
Lieutenant Fordham was in poor shape – all
that he could tell me was that Private Hedley
had struck him. His forehead appeared to be
bleeding and it looked as if he had been   30
hit on the mouth.

MAJOR   Thank you, Captain Knox. I would now like to
call upon the medical orderly, Mr Joseph
Hines, who attended Lieutenant Fordham at
the dressing station. Mr Hines, please give   35
us your evidence.

ORDERLY   I examined Lieutenant Fordham on his
admittance. As well as the considerable
damage to his leg, he appeared to have been
struck on the head. The marks associated   40
with this injury were consistent with a blow
dealt by a fist.

MAJOR   Thank you, Mr Hines. Is Lieutenant Fordham
able to give evidence?

ORDERLY   No Sir, he suffered an amputation to his   45
right leg and will be invalided home. He's in
pretty poor shape, Sir.

MAJOR   Thank you. *(shuffles his papers)* Private Hedley,
this court martial is at an end. You will be
returned to custody whilst we examine   50

the evidence and submit it to Field Marshal Sir John French. You will be informed of your sentence within the next twenty-eight days.

All but Tom exit.

Scene 11

June, 1915

A small room in the barracks. Tom is alone.

TOM Mother, Jenny … all the things I wrote for you – they got lost in the explosion. I don't suppose they'll let me send you anything now and I don't know what they'll tell you about me and what happened … *(he sinks*   5 *to his knees, holding his head, trying not to cry)* I'm frightened! *(long pause)* They're going to shoot me tomorrow … cowardice, insubordination *(he buries his head in his hands again)* What does it feel like?   10 Being shot? And then, just not being anything anymore? *(he is suddenly still – stands up)* I didn't know what to say to them about Will – how Mattie and me tried to stop him giving the game away. I thought *he'd*   15 tell them the truth – I didn't want to tell tales meself. Then I realised what was going to happen to me and I tried to explain. They just don't believe me. *(he shouts out)* It's not fair! It's not fair! *(he buries his face in his*   20 *hands again. Pause. He raises his head, calmer)* All right then. I'm remembering me dad. I'm telling meself I'm going to Heaven and I'll

see him soon. I'll just pretend I died in the
explosion with Mattie and the other Byford
lads – that's it. When they put the   25
blindfold round me, I'll wait for the explosion
and remember – it's a privilege to die for me
country!

*Captain Knox and the Orderly enter and lead Tom
forward. Captain Knox pins a white piece of paper on
his chest. The Orderly puts a scarf round his eyes.*

CAPTAIN KNOX Take aim. *(pause)* Fire!

*Sound of gunfire. Tom drops to the ground.
Blackout.*

Scene 12

July, 1915

*A street in Byford village. Hannah enters, cuddling
her baby, humming the nursery rhyme, 'Rock-a-
bye baby'. Polly and Lizzie enter to stand at side
of stage. Their voices overlap and they are not
their usual jeering selves.*

POLLY Have you heard—

LIZZIE Did you see—

POLLY They're bringing telegrams—

LIZZIE Me Uncle Harry—

POLLY All of 'em killed – all the Byford lads –   5
wiped out together.

LIZZIE Me Uncle Harry – Mam won't stop crying.
They've opened the church – they're
bringing flowers.

POLLY   Twenty of 'em! 10

LIZZIE   Jack Ellis down the lane.

POLLY   Not him from the Hall—

LIZZIE   No, but they say he's lost a leg.

POLLY   Everyone else. Maybe Mattie Clark too?

LIZZIE   Mattie Clark! See if *she* knows ... *(gesturing* 15
to Hannah)

*As they approach Hannah, Mrs Hedley and Jenny
Lucas enter with a telegram. Jenny hands it to
Hannah. Hannah reads it silently. The telegram is
read aloud by Captain Knox entering at the other
side of the stage.*

CAPTAIN KNOX   'Madam, It is my painful duty to inform you
that a report has this day been received from
the War Office notifying the death of
Number 2575, Private M. J. Clark, which
occurred abroad – locality not stated – 20
on the 20th May, 1915, and I am to express to
you the sympathy and regret of the Army
Council at your loss. The cause of death was
Killed in Action.'

HANNAH   This isn't happening. He didn't even see 25
the baby. He didn't see our little boy.

*Mrs Hedley takes the baby from Hannah. Hannah
and Jenny embrace.*

LIZZIE   There's been no telegram for her – Ma Hedley.
Tom Hedley's alive – the only one.

POLLY   How's he the only one? Did he run away?

Polly and Lizzie sidle up to Jenny, who turns on them.

JENNY L	What do you mean – did he run away?	30

LIZZIE   You heard me, Jenny Lucas. If he's alive and all
the others are dead he must have scarpered.

MRS HEDLEY   *(turning to Polly and Lizzie)* Get off with you! You
make yerself useful, Polly Watkins. And Lizzie
Palmer, shouldn't you be helping yer mam   35
if yer uncle's dead? *(Polly and Lizzie exit. To
Hannah)* Hannah, lass – Shall I take little John
in for his sleep?

HANNAH   *(she fights back tears)* No, Mrs Hedley. You get
along now. See if you can find out what's   40
happened to your Tom. I'll be all right,
honest I will. And if I'm not, I'm in good
company, that's for sure. There's three of us
down this row with men killed. No, you get
off now. If Tom's been spared, Mattie …   45
Mattie would have been glad – I'll try to be
too … *(she runs off with the baby, in tears)*

*Polly and Lizzie enter again. They are their old
jeering selves.*

POLLY   Have they heard yet?

LIZZIE   Can't have done.

POLLY   Mebbe they have – maybe that's why they   50
daren't show their faces down the street.

JENNY L   Why don't you come right out with it and tell
me what you want to say!

LIZZIE   Oh, you'll hear soon enough.

POLLY   We know why you haven't got a telegram   55
yet.

LIZZIE   You will get one – but what will it say?

Enter Dr Lindsay.

DR LINDSAY   Mrs Hedley, Jenny Lucas. *(nodding curtly to Polly
              and Lizzie, who exit reluctantly)* Good day to
              you. *(to Mrs Hedley and Jenny)* May I have a   60
              word?

MRS HEDLEY   Dr Lindsay, do you know something? Have you
              heard something about Tom?

DR LINDSAY   There's been news from his Lordship at the
              Hall. You've maybe heard. Will Fordham –   65
              Master Will – got out alive. He's lost a leg.
              He's still in a field hospital over there.
              They're bringing him out soon. *(hands over a
              telegram from his pocket)* Now I'm giving you
              this, I think it's about Tom. I've heard   70
              rumours to do with him and Will, and
              I thought I'd better be here.

              *Captain Knox reads aloud from the side of the
              stage.*

CAPTAIN KNOX 'I am directed to inform you that a report has
              been received from the War Office to the
              effect that No. 2576, Private T. E. Hedley,   75
              was sentenced to suffer death by being shot,
              after being tried by Court Martial for striking
              a superior officer. His sentence was duly
              executed on 1st July, 1915.' *(exit Captain Knox)*

MRS HEDLEY   He was only seventeen!   80

DR LINDSAY   They say he struck Will Fordham and tried to
              run away.

Scene 13

July, 1915

*Byford village. The Vicar enters. Hannah, Polly and
Lizzie stand on one side facing Jenny Lucas and
Mrs Hedley. Hannah is carrying her baby. Some of
the villagers stand by Hannah's side.*

VICAR Dearly beloved, we are gathered today to
honour the memory of the brave young men
of Byford who died on 20th May, 1915, that
England may live. We commend their souls
to the love of our Heavenly Father, who will 5
keep them until that day when we will meet
them again, never to be parted. We also pray
for the speedy recovery of William Fordham
of Byford Hall, who has sustained such
terrible injuries in the defence of our 10
glorious Empire. *(exit Vicar)*

JENNY L Mrs Hedley, he couldn't have done it – Mrs
Hedley! Surely he couldn't …

MRS HEDLEY I don't know anything any more.

HANNAH Well, I hope you're proud of yourself, 15
Jenny Lucas. If it hadn't been for your Tom
Hedley, Mattie would never have joined up.
And Tom Hedley thinking he was such a big
man – meddling in what he couldn't cope
with. And now look at what's happened! 20

JENNY L Hannah, please!

HANNAH Don't you 'please' me.

JENNY L I've lost someone as well!

HANNAH Someone? He's a beast – he's not a person.

JENNY L   I've lost Tom just like you've lost Mattie!   25

HANNAH   You weren't married to him and you'd only known him six months! You tell me you're sorry he killed all those men and tell me you wish you hadn't met him. Then I might think about forgiving you.   30

JENNY L   But I don't know if it's all true!

HANNAH   Right then – you and I are finished! Don't you ever come back here, and don't you dare try to touch my baby ever again.

Hannah walks away. Polly and Lizzie join her. Hannah, Polly, Lizzie and the Villagers all shout.

VOICE 1   Go on!   35

VOICE 2   Get out!

VOICE 3   Get out of this village!

VOICE 4   Don't show yer face again!

VOICE 5   Go on, Jenny Lucas!

VOICE 6   Murderer! He was a murderer!   40

JENNY L   No!

MRS HEDLEY   *(puts arm round her)* Come on, lass. We're not wanted here. *(Dr Lindsay enters)*

DR LINDSAY   Mrs Hedley, Jenny. Let me help you.

Everyone except for Jenny Lucas, Mrs Hedley and Dr Lindsay exit, looking back and muttering to each other in a hostile way.

DR LINDSAY   I'm buying a practice about fifty miles from here. I'll be needing a housekeeper, and someone to help me with the books. What about you both coming with me?   45

Please let me help. I feel responsible. I was
there in the recruiting station and my   50
signature helped to send those lads off to
France – to their deaths.

MRS HEDLEY   What do you think, Jenny?

JENNY L   You're all the family I've got left now, Mrs Hedley!

*Exit Dr Lindsay, Jenny Lucas and Mrs Hedley,
together.*

Scene 14

The present day

*In the Clarks' kitchen, Jenny Clark is talking on her
mobile phone.*

JENNY C   Sarah – I've found some great stuff here for the
project! Lots of diaries and letters and things.
My great granddad – he was called Mattie
Clark – was killed in 1915 – in France. This
place called Hill 60. I checked on that war   5
memorial outside school, and his name's
there. Then it gets a bit confused 'cos there's
Jenny Lucas who was my great granny's
sister. Now, here's the gory bit! Tom Hedley –
that was her sweetheart – got executed by   10
a firing squad for getting my great granddad
and all his mates killed. And Tom's name
isn't on the memorial at all. Oh, I forgot the
really odd bit! Just after this Tom Hedley
died, or got shot or whatever, Jenny Lucas   15
starts calling herself Jenny Hedley – just as if
she really had been married to him. Her
diary says that my great granny, Hannah –

that was Mattie's widow – didn't want
anything more to do with her when she   20
found out about Tom Hedley … No, they
never ever met again! That's some quarrel!
I mean, they were sisters … Anyway, I've still
got some more stuff to look at. There's a
letter from Hannah's son, John – that's my   25
grandad – and he's writing to his mum, that's
Hannah, my great granny. The date's 1941 –
that's the same time as the next war, the
Second World War.

Jenny Clark walks off stage.

Scene 15

May, 1941

*Jenny Hedley is sitting on a train with a small bag
on her knee. John Clark enters. He has a large
suitcase. An older Hannah observes the scene.*

HANNAH   'Walsham, 8th May, 1941. Dear Mother, this is
to reassure you that I'm all right after the
raid on the station here last week. Now,
I don't know how to tell you this, but
something very strange happened when   5
I was in the train coming back …'

JOHN   Is this seat taken?

JENNY H   Not as far as I know.

John looks dubiously up at the luggage rack.

JOHN   I think I'll just leave it on the floor! *(sits. Brief
silence)*

JENNY H   Are you going to Walsham as well?   10

JOHN	Yes. Just been transferred. I take it you're stationed there?
JENNY H	Radio operative. I've been there since the start of the war. And you?
JOHN	Navigator. *(another brief silence)* So you've been home on leave? 15
JENNY H	A very short one. Family wedding in Lakeley.
JOHN	Oh, nice. Who was it?
JENNY H	Funnily enough, my mum – well, my adopted mum. She and her boss decided to get 20 married after over … oh, twenty years. He's the local doctor and she's been his housekeeper since about 1919.
JOHN	That must feel odd for you.
JENNY H	Well, no. I'm really pleased. She's been 25 widowed since 1908 so she deserves a bit of happiness, I reckon.
JOHN	Well, yes, indeed. Good luck to them both! I wish my mum had married again. She was widowed in 1915. *(another brief silence)* Are 30 you married?
JENNY H	No, I never was. My sweetheart was killed in the last war too, and no one ever measured up to him, really. What about you?
JOHN	Yes, we've been married over a year … 35 Actually I'm just longing to tell someone! I found out yesterday my wife's expecting our first baby!
JENNY H	Oh, congratulations! That must be really exciting.
JOHN	I think my mum's almost more excited 40 than Rachel and me.

JENNY H	You'll have to tell me how things go. I feel a bit flat now the wedding's over.
JOHN	I expect Walsham's a big station. Will you give me your name so I can look you up? 45
JENNY H	It's Jenny Hedley.
JOHN	Mine's John Clark.
JENNY H	*(slowly)* John Clark? Are you from Byford by any chance?
JOHN	That's right. Joicey Row. 50
JENNY H	I don't suppose your mother's name is Hannah?
JOHN	*(surprised)* Yes, it is.
JENNY H	And your father was Mattie Clark?
JOHN	Yes – but I never knew him. He was killed two weeks before I was born. 55
JENNY H	A tunnelling explosion? 20th May, 1915?
JOHN	That's right, in France. Hill 60. How do you know all this?

(Hannah continues to read the letter)

HANNAH	'So there she was, mum – my Auntie Jenny! Obviously I asked her why I had never 60 heard about her before and she said – she was very tactful – that there had been a terrible misunderstanding. Just then we stopped at a station and it was obvious the train was going to be crowded out at any 65 minute. We arranged to meet next week, in the mess perhaps, and she promised she'd explain – try to sort the misunderstanding out. She said she was glad she'd met me – that she'd been longing to see me ever 70 since I'd been a month old …'

John approaches Hannah as Jenny Hedley exits.

JOHN   We never met again, mum. She was killed in that raid.

Hannah runs into his embrace. He hugs her.

HANNAH   I never said how much I really loved her.

JOHN   I'm sure she knew you did, deep down.   75

HANNAH   How could you know that? You only met her once!

JOHN   I found out the address of her adopted mum and I wrote to her …

HANNAH   *(wiping her eyes)* I know – Tom Hedley's   80
mam …

JOHN   And she and her husband, Dr … Dr …

HANNAH   … Lindsay, I think he was called …

JOHN   That's right. Well, they came up to get her stuff
to take back to Lakeley, and they gave me   85
bundles of letters and diaries and things. Mrs
Lindsay said Jenny would have wanted her
birth family to have them all. But Mum, there
was one thing I found out from them.
Something that Jenny *hadn't* written down.   90
I made a note of it myself before I forgot. Dr
Lindsay said it was something that happened
in the great flu epidemic at the end of the
Great War.

HANNAH   1919. Half of what was left of the village   95
was sick. Lots died.

Exit Hannah and John.

Scene 16

April, 1919

Dr Lindsay's house. Jenny Lucas is reading. Dr Lindsay enters with his doctor's bag.

DR LINDSAY   Jenny, Mrs Hedley! Quickly!

Mrs Hedley enters from the other side of the stage.

MRS HEDLEY   Dinner isn't cooked yet, sir.

DR LINDSAY   No, I'm not interested in the dinner. Jenny, put the book away – there's something far more important! I've been up to Byford. I got   5 a message from the Hall – Will Fordham died this afternoon.

MRS HEDLEY   Oh, poor lad! Was it the influenza?

DR LINDSAY   It was indeed. He hadn't much resistance to anything since he got back from France.   10

MRS HEDLEY   I'm not surprised he was in low spirits. Losing his leg.

DR LINDSAY   I think his mood over the past three years might have had something to do with what he told me last week when he first got   15 ill – something in the nature of a confessional.

Scene 17

April, 1919

Byford Hall. Will is sitting down, pulling a rug over his knees. Dr Lindsay is next to him with his bag, holding his stethoscope.

DR LINDSAY   Right then, I've sounded your chest – it could be a lot worse. And that stump of yours

seems to have healed nicely. How do you feel
in yourself, Will?

WILL   Not exactly ready for the hunt, Doctor. Not   5
that I ever did!

DR LINDSAY   Take it easy. Influenza's not something to be
trifled with. Get plenty to eat. Build up your
strength.

WILL   What for? Picking up my bed and walking?   10
Oh, I'm sorry! It's not your fault.

DR LINDSAY   Well, it's hardly yours, lad.

WILL   Oh yes, I think it is.

DR LINDSAY   Come on, now. I've heard the reports. Massive
explosion. You didn't stand a chance.   15
(silence) So just try to look forward to the
summer now that the war's over. Start slowly.
Sit out in the fresh air a bit. You never know
what you'll be getting up to soon if you've a
mind to it.   20

WILL   That's rather the point, Doctor. *If* I've a mind to it.

DR LINDSAY   No one can just tell you to look on the bright
side. Heavens! If it was me and somebody
said that, I'd probably land them one! But
seriously, Will, if you fret like this you'll do   25
yourself no good. Tell you what. I'll look out
some books. Send you over something to
read. *(silence)* Bye lad, I'll see you tomorrow.

WILL   Doctor!

DR LINDSAY   What is it?   30

WILL   It *is* my fault. Not just the leg, I mean, 'C'
company ... all the Byford lads. All those
families left behind ... I've got to tell you

something … I must tell you what really
happened.   35

DR LINDSAY All right then. Take your time. Slowly lad.

WILL I did try, Doctor. I think I was a decent officer
for a bit. But deep down I was always
terrified, and then I just couldn't take any
more. Quite suddenly, I mean. It was that   40
day after we lost Will Casey and John Baker.
We could hear them out there in No Man's
Land, crying out to us. I don't suppose they
knew what they were saying anymore. But
we knew. We heard them call out to their   45
pals, to the lads who'd shared a desk at
school, who'd fought in scraps with them
and wolf-whistled the girls and kissed their
mothers goodbye and told their dads they'd
make them proud. And the men, looking at   50
me as if they expected me to make it all right
again. But I couldn't. And they died –
frightened, alone, such pain! *(silence)* Mattie
Clark, Tom Hedley – two of the best lads I've
ever met … oh God, what have I done!   55
Tom Hedley – it wasn't his fault he struck
me, it was mine. I was out for the count for
days. I didn't even know about the charge
against Tom till I got back to England, to the
nursing home. I certainly didn't hear about   60
the – the execution. Please, please believe me!

Scene 18

April, 1919

Dr Lindsay's house. Jenny Lucas and Mrs Hedley stand with Dr Lindsay, shocked.

DR LINDSAY Apparently he lost his nerve completely in one of the tunnels he was checking up on with Tom and Mattie. He said he was in danger of giving away their position. Tom and Mattie both decided they 5 had to knock him out to shut him up, but it was too late – the enemy heard them. Tossed in a grenade. The tunnel collapsed. End of 'C' Company.

JENNY L So it wasn't Tom's fault! 10

DR LINDSAY No indeed. Will insisted that the cowardice was his own, not Tom's. But I felt I just couldn't tell you till now, till poor Will had died.

MRS HEDLEY But why didn't Tom tell them the truth?

DR LINDSAY Heaven knows. 15

JENNY L Will was his friend. It would be like telling tales.

MRS HEDLEY They weren't in the playground! This was life and death!

DR LINDSAY In any case, Tom was just a private. I don't honestly think his word would have been 20 accepted. No, the only chance might have been if Will had owned up.

JENNY L And he didn't even know Tom had been charged. I think I feel sorry for Will!

DR LINDSAY Look, I've a plan. I'm going wait till a decent 25 period of mourning is over, and then I'm

going to speak to Lord Fordham. There's no
need to blacken Will's name after all this
time. We can get together and make up some
other story that would explain why Tom   30
hit Will without dishonouring either of them,
and why it had taken Will so long to
remember it all. If Lord Fordham spreads
this story round the village …

MRS HEDLEY   No! No, Dr Lindsay. It would still be a lie.   35
Tom is at peace and we know the truth in
our hearts. That's enough.

DR LINDSAY   What about you, Jenny. What do *you* think?

JENNY L   *(pause)* I'd love for that Polly and Lizzie to know
the truth, but I don't suppose they'd ever   40
admit it even if we told them! And I just don't
think Hannah'll ever believe what really
happened. Mrs Hedley's right – let's leave
things as they are.

Exit Dr Lindsay, Jenny Lucas and Mrs Hedley.

Scene 19

The present day

*The Clarks' kitchen. Jenny Clark and Mrs Clark are
putting the papers and books back in the trunk.*

MRS CLARK   Have we got it all sorted out now, do you think?

JENNY C   I can't wait to tell them all at school. Maybe
they'll put Tom's name on the war memorial
with all the others. That would be brilliant!
I feel a bit odd, though – having his   5
surname in my name, and everything. That

was my dad, wasn't it? The baby that Granny
Rachel was expecting?

MRS CLARK Yes. And I suppose in the end your great
granny Hannah must have accepted what   10
the Doctor said. She must have forgiven Tom.

JENNY C But there wasn't anything to forgive!

MRS CLARK Well, no! But they didn't have the right
information to go on at the time, did they?
Anyway, I think everyone must have been   15
happy to call your dad Roger Hedley Clark,
and they did it as much in memory of Jenny
as of Tom.

JENNY C Because she loved him so much …

MRS CLARK Yes, and because she was so loyal.   20

*Mrs Clark and Jenny Clark exit, carrying the trunk
between them.*

Scene 20

The present day

*All characters are present. Will, Mattie and Tom
stand side by side.*

1ST TEACHER Today – 11th November – is a very special
Remembrance Day at Byford High School.
Some of our students have been looking
back at those of their great grandparents
who took part in the Great War between   5
1914 and 1919.

2ND TEACHER Forty-five men of Byford died as a result of that
war. Twenty of them were killed on one day
– 20th May, 1915, in France. Every day near

the school gate we pass a memorial on   10
which their names are inscribed. But there is
one notable exception – the name of Tom
Hedley is not on that memorial. Today, we
want to set the record straight.

JENNY C   Tom Hedley would still have been at school   15
if he'd been alive today – he was only
seventeen. They thought he was a coward
and they shot him.

HANNAH   But we've found out that really – in spite of
everything that was said about him at the   20
time – he was a very, very brave soldier.

JENNY L   *(moves forward)* Sometimes in the summer, at
dawn or just before – about when *it* must
have happened – I can't sleep. I get out of
bed, throw a few clothes on and go off   25
down the lane for some air. It's lovely then.
There's wild roses in the hedgerows. I pull a
branch towards me and hold me head up to
the petals. There's just the faintest smell.
Sometimes I think it's the scent of all the   30
wonderful things that would have happened
for me and Tom if he had still been here. It's
such a faint, faint smell – no one would know
it was there, just me. Just like no one knows
how much he's still here, in me heart. All   35
the good things that happen – I tell him all
about them. I've got to do all the living for
both of us now.

DR LINDSAY *(quoting)* 'They shall not grow old, as we that
are left grow old: 40
Age shall not weary them, nor the years
condemn.

	At the going down of the sun and in the morning	
	We will remember them.'	45
HANNAH	*(as if reading from the War Memorial)* Matthew John Clark …	
STUDENT 1	Edward Hubert Watkins …	
ORDERLY	*(overlapping)* John Watson …	
STUDENT 2	*(as before)* Harold Wood …	50
MRS CLARK	Lawrence Tennant …	
STUDENT 3	Ronald James White …	
VICAR	William Casey …	
STUDENT 4	Alexander Casey …	
MRS HEDLEY	Joseph George Robson …	55
STUDENT 5	Christopher Hodge …	
MILKMAN	Frederick William Christie …	
STUDENT 6	Henry Baker …	
POLLY	Robert William Charlton …	
STUDENT 7	Joseph Southwood Stephenson …	60
LORD FORDHAM	Robert Clive Daniels …	
STUDENT 8	Willoughby George May …	
LIZZIE	Harold Palmer …	
STUDENT 9	Stanley Wilson …	
DR LINDSAY	Albert Garrick …	65
STUDENT 10	Frederick Alan Peterson …	
JENNY C AND JENNY L	Thomas Edward Hedley.	

Activities

Activity 1: The play's setting

Act One Scene 1 takes place in 1914. Act One Scene 2 takes place in the present day. This activity asks you to perform these two scenes in order to explore the contrasts and links between them.

a **In groups,** read Act One Scene 1 aloud (there are five characters). Now talk about how the characters' way of life and the language they use show that the scene is set in the past.

Now act out the scene as if you were rehearsing to perform it on stage. Before you start, share ideas about:
- a suitable costume for each character
- essential props
- moves and positions on stage
- accents.

b **In pairs,** read Act One Scene 2 aloud. Now talk about how the following aspects of the scene show that it is set in the present:
- the characters' way of life
- the language the characters use.

Now act out the scene as if you were rehearsing to perform it on stage. Make the same preparations as you did for Scene 1.

c **As a class,** use what you have learned from your performances to consider why *White Poppies* begins with scenes set in different times. Think about:
- any links you have spotted between the characters
- how the plot might develop from this point
- your knowledge of World War I.

Activity 2: Jenny Lucas and Tom Hedley: growing close

This activity asks you to trace and write about the friendship between Jenny Lucas and Tom Hedley as it develops in Act One Scenes 3, 5, 7 and 8. You will also collect information about their characters and background to understand future events in the play.

a **In groups,** read Act One Scenes 3, 5, 7 and 8 aloud. (Read Scenes 4 and 6 silently). Jenny and Tom appear in each scene; you will also need readers for Will Fordham, Lizzie and Mrs Hedley.

b **As a class,** discuss how these scenes set during September and October 1914 show Jenny and Tom growing close to each other. Make a chart like the one below to record key moments in their friendship.

Scene	Quotation	What the quotation shows
3	**Jenny:** '… none of the other lasses will talk to me yet'	Jenny is isolated and lonely at Byford Hall: she needs friends of her own age
5	**Tom:** 'If you'd like to come and see us at the shop…'	
7	*Tom is showing Jenny a box*	
8	**Jenny:** 'I'd like to walk out with you, Tom Hedley'	

Use your completed chart to consider the things Jenny and Tom find they have in common. Why do these help to draw them together?

c **By yourself,** write an account of how and why Jenny and Tom are attracted to one another in this part of the play. You should write four paragraphs, one about each scene you have read, and use the Point–Evidence–Explanation method of analysis.

Activity 3: Taking the King's shilling

This activity asks you to read Act One Scenes 9, 11 and 12 to explore why Mattie Clark and Tom Hedley enlist in the army. You will then write an exchange of letters from Mattie to his wife Hannah in April 1915, showing how they both feel about him 'joining up' to fight in World War I.

a **In pairs,** read Act One Scene 9 aloud. Now talk about how this scene brings out:
   • the close friendship between Mattie and Tom
   • why Mattie has been thinking of going to fight in France.

b **In groups,** share your ideas from your work in **a** above. Now read Act One Scene 11 aloud. You will need readers for Mattie, the Vicar, Lizzie, Polly, Hannah and Jenny Lucas.

   List four or five reasons why Mattie decides to enlist. Decide on their order of importance to *him*, justifying your decisions from the text.

c **As a class,** read Act One Scene 12 aloud. You will need readers for Mattie, Tom and Jenny Lucas. Now talk about:
   • why Tom decides to join up
   • Jenny's feelings about his decision.

   With which character do your own sympathies lie?

d **By yourself,** write two letters. The first is from Mattie to Hannah when he gets to France; the second is Hannah's reply.

You should use the scenes you have read, and your own imagination, to bring out the feelings of Mattie and Hannah. Express these in a suitable style, drawing on your knowledge of each character.

Activity 4: The language of persuasion

This activity asks you to look closely at the language the Vicar uses in Act One Scene 11 to persuade the young men to go and fight in the war. You will go on to write a short pamphlet about today's armed forces.

a **In pairs,** read the Vicar's sermon in Act One Scene 11 aloud and the words of the hymn 'I vow to thee, my country'. Now consider how the language of these is persuasive and emotive. What feelings does it appeal to? Would it have prompted *you* to join up in 1915?

Think in particular about the effect of these phrases:
- '...to help our French allies against the common enemy.'
- '...it will be their duty to set an example...'
- '...to do his duty by his country...'
- 'The love that never falters, the love that pays the price,
- The love that makes undaunted the final sacrifice'
- '...here is his opportunity. There may be no others!'

b **As a class,** share your ideas from your work in **a** above. Now imagine you are in charge of recruiting young people for today's army, navy or airforce. Talk about how you would encourage them to enlist. What similarities and differences would there be to 1915 in:
- your message
- your use of language?

c **By yourself,** plan and produce a two-page recruiting pamphlet for the modern armed services **or** a two-page pamphlet by a pacifist group discouraging young people from joining up. It should include:
- persuasive language likely to appeal to young people
- short quotations from men and women on active service
- a range of presentational devices.

Activity 5: Going off to war

This activity asks you to read Act One Scenes 13, 14 and 15, then produce a local newspaper report about the Byford lads going off to war.

a **In groups,** read Act One Scene 13 aloud. You will need readers for Mattie, Tom, the Recruiting Officer and Dr Lindsay. Now talk about how the events of this scene might be reported in a local newspaper in February 1915. Are there any details the newspaper might leave out? Which points do you think the newspaper might want to highlight?

b **In pairs,** read the dialogue between Dr Lindsay and Jenny Lucas in Act One Scene 14 aloud. Now talk about Dr Lindsay's attitude towards 'brave young men like Tom signing up'. Why does he support Tom's decision? How might his views be reported in a newspaper in 1915?

c **As a class,** read Act One Scene 15 aloud. You will need readers for Jenny Lucas, Mrs Hedley and Tom. Now choose someone to role-play Mrs Hedley. Put her in the hot seat: your aim is to uncover her private feelings about her 16-year-old son going off to war. Will her feelings be mixed or all of one kind?

d **By yourself,** imagine you are a journalist on the *Byford Bugle*. Write a front-page story about Mattie, Tom and the other village boys setting off for war. It should include two interviews with local people. Your headline and sub-headline could be:

> ## BYFORD LADS OFF TO SERVE KING AND COUNTRY!
>
> Emotional scenes as village volunteers head for war

Activity 6: Present and past: how might they be linked?

This activity asks you to look through the present-day scenes in Act One and work out possible links between Jenny Clark and the characters from 1914–1915. You will then develop your ideas by improvising a scene of your own.

a **In groups,** re-read the present-day scenes in Act One – Scenes 2, 6 and 10. Now read Scene 16 and decide what hints it gives about future events.

b **As a class,** compile a question chart about possible links between the Clark family in the present day and characters from the past. It could begin like this:

Present day	1914–1915	Questions about the links
Jenny's surname is Clark	Hannah marries Mattie Clark	How might Jenny Clark be related to Mattie and Hannah?
Jenny's middle name is Hedley	Tom and his mother are called Hedley	
Jenny's dead father was called Roger Hedley Clark	Tom and Mattie are best friends	

Try to create at least six questions.

c **In groups,** choose **one** question from your list. Plan an improvisation that provides some answers to it. It can take place at any time from 1914 onwards. You are free to introduce any characters you like – those already in the play and/or those you imagine.

Perform your improvisation in front of another group. Listen to their comments on how successful it was. Then watch and comment on theirs.

Activity 7: Girls in conflict

This activity asks you to perform Act Two Scene 2 to bring out and explain the friction between Jenny Lucas, Polly and Lizzie. You will explore this scene as if you were preparing it for a stage performance.

a **In groups,** read Act Two Scene 2 aloud. You will need readers for Jenny, Polly and Lizzie. Ask another group member to act as director.

Talk about how to perform this scene for an audience at a school production of the play. Carefully consider:
- what you want to show of Jenny's character and feelings
- what you want to emphasise about Polly and Lizzie
- whether the scene should be mainly comic or mainly serious
- what moves and actions on stage will bring the scene to life.

Try out your interpretations by acting the scene in different ways.

b **As a class,** share your ideas from your work in **a** above. Take into account the playwright's notes on the three characters concerned:

Jenny: *Whoever plays Jenny's part has to balance her vulnerability with her strength of character.*

Polly and Lizzie: *Work out how they behave together as a comic duo (with sinister overtones) and decide just how much one is the leader and one the follower.*

Finally, look closely at the text to decide whether Polly and Lizzie are jealous of Jenny or just cruel bullies. How will you bring out your interpretation in performance?

c **In groups,** perform this scene (books in hands) as realistically as you can in front of another group. You should then act as an audience for their performance.

Activity 8: Tragedy in the tunnel

This activity asks you to write director's notes on Act Two Scenes 5, 7, 8 and 9, to bring out their dramatic qualities and reveal the characters of Mattie, Tom and Will Fordham to the audience.

a **As a class,** read Act Two Scenes 5, 7, 8 and 9 straight through. Now talk about how the playwright wants the audience to respond to them. What impressions of fighting in World War I should these scenes give? Are the characters shown to be heroic, pitiable or both? Is the action exciting, horrific or both?

b **In groups,** copy and complete the chart below about the characters of Mattie, Tom and Will in this part of the play. Include at least three more points about each character, illustrated by quotations.

Mattie	Tom	Will
Fond of a joke: 'She might if she finds out about the lice in your tunic!'	Eager for action: 'What about the enemy? Do you see much of them?'	Weighed down by responsibility: 'I sometimes don't think I can...'

c **As a class,** compare your charts from the group work. Now talk about the main *mood* of each of these scenes. As the director, how would you bring out for an audience:
  • the *suspense* in this part of the play
  • exactly what happens at the climax of the action in Scene 8?

d **By yourself,** imagine you are producing these scenes for an amateur theatre group. Make notes about:
  • how Mattie, Tom and Will react to danger in different ways
  • how to represent the bunker and the tunnel on stage
  • how to bring out the tension and drama of the events.

Include brief comments about the set, the lighting and the sound effects you plan to use.

Activity 9: Tom: coward or hero?

This activity asks you to compare and contrast different characters' reactions to what they hear about Tom in Act Two Scenes 12 and 13. You will go on to write a speech about his court martial and execution.

a **As a class,** read Act Two Scenes 10, 11, 12 and 13 aloud. Now talk about why Tom is court-martialled and shot at dawn. Could he have been spared his fate? If so, how?

b **In groups,** look closely at Scenes 12 and 13. Copy and complete the chart below to show how different characters in Byford feel about Tom.

Characters	Reaction to the news about Tom
Polly & Lizzie	think he is a coward who ran away and left his friends to die
Jenny Lucas	
Mrs Hedley	
Hannah	
Dr Lindsay	

Take each character's reaction in turn. Show how far you sympathise with them by creating a scale of 1 to 3, where 1 = 'don't sympathise at all', 2 = 'sympathise to some extent' and 3 = 'fully sympathise'. Justify your opinions.

c **By yourself,** imagine you are a Byford villager who does not appear in the play. There is a meeting at the Village Hall after Scene 13 to decide whether to honour Tom as a hero or condemn him as a coward. You have found out from an officer home on leave the full facts about what happened in the tunnel.

Write the speech you will make at the village meeting.

Activity 10: An obituary for Will Fordham

This activity asks you to use information from the whole play to write an obituary for Will Fordham in *The Times*. It will include comments from people who knew him.

a **As a class,** read two or three obituaries from daily newspapers, including, if possible, one for a person who died young. Draw up a list of the main features of obituaries and analyse the style in which they are written.

b **In groups,** read Act Two Scenes 17 and 18. Now plan *The Times* obituary for Will Fordham on 30 April 1919.

 Look back through the play and note down the main *facts* it gives about Will's life and death. Include details about:
 • his family and their status in Byford
 • Will's interests as a young man
 • how World War I changed his plans for his future
 • how he came to be wounded and invalided home
 • how he died and at what age.

c **In pairs,** talk about the impressions of Will's *personality* you get from:
 • Act One Scenes 3, 4 and 5
 • Act Two Scenes 5, 7, 8 and 9.

 How do you judge his character on the evidence of these scenes?

d **By yourself,** think carefully about Act Two Scenes 17 and 18. Dr Lindsay says 'There's no need to blacken Will's name after all this time'. Do you agree?

Now write a three-paragraph obituary for Will. It should be mainly factual but you should include some opinions about him – for example, from Jenny, Mrs Hedley, Dr Lindsay or a fellow officer. Remember to use suitable language and style for the time.

Activity 11: Plotboarding the play

This activity asks you to choose six key events from the play, then to present them in graphic form. A 'plotboard' is made up of frames set out in chronological order. Each one contains a sketch of the event it describes, a caption and (where appropriate) speech bubbles.

a **In pairs,** talk about what you consider to be the play's central event.

- The young men going off to war?
- Mattie's death?
- Tom's execution?
- The Remembrance Day ceremony in Byford?
- Jenny's loss?
- The family's quarrel?

Argue strongly for your opinion.

Now select five other key events in the play that link up with the one you have chosen as 'central'. Explain to each other the reasons for your choices, even if these are the same.

b **By yourself,** draw six square frames on a large sheet of paper. In each, sketch what you want it to show. Add one-sentence captions written in the third person and speech (or thought) bubbles written in the first person (these can be quotations from the text).

Test the success of your plotboard by showing it to someone who has not read the play. Can they follow it clearly? If not, make the necessary changes.

Produce the final version of your plotboard in a striking and attractive way.

Activity 12: White poppies

This activity asks you to look over the whole play and explain why the playwright chose the title *White poppies*. You will need to conduct research about soldiers who were shot for cowardice in World War I and link this with the play's themes.

a **As a class,** talk about why red poppies are:
   • associated with World War I
   • used as symbols of remembrance for those who died in this and other wars.

   Do you agree that:
   • we should observe Remembrance Day on 11 November every year?
   • red poppies are the most appropriate symbols?

b **By yourself,**
   • carry out research into the Poppies for Peace movement by visiting www.heinemann.co.uk/hotlinks.
   • You could also find out about soldiers who were 'shot at dawn' for cowardice in World War I.

c **As a class,** share your findings.
   • What is your own attitude to Poppies for Peace?
   • There are still over 300 British soldiers who were 'shot at dawn' in World War I and have not been officially pardoned. Give your views about whether they should be.

d **In groups,** draw on the research you have done to consider why the playwright calls her play *White poppies*. Which scenes make a strong case for seeing Tom as a brave soldier rather than a coward? How does the play's structure emphasise this theme?

e **By yourself,** write a formal literature essay about the meaning of the title and how well, in your opinion, the play reflects it. Support the points you make with quotations and detailed comments on them.

Glossary

any road anyhow

Archduke Archduke Franz Ferdinand, heir to the throne of Austria and Hungary, was assassinated, and this event led to the start of the First World War

bairn baby

bait box lunchbox

billeted sleeping

blighty one a lucky injury; a serious but not fatal wound that would result in your being sent home to Britain to recuperate

the Blitz the bombing campaign waged against London by the German Airforce during the Second World War

cabbie cab or taxi driver

cack-handed clumsy, not practical

canaries canaries were taken into mines to alert the miners to gas leaks. The birds were sensitive to gas and they passed out from breathing it in, so the men knew they were in danger

champion brilliant

condensed milk tinned, sweetened milk from which the water has been removed to help it keep longer

evensong evening church service

gent gentleman

grand brilliant

grub food

hanky panky inappropriate behaviour

honour at the start of a country dance men bow and ladies curtsey to their partners as a mark of courtesy

Hun the German Army

jabbering on excessive or meaningless chat

Jerry a British name for the German soldiers

lass girl

lay the charge set up the explosives

leave authorised time away from a regiment, holiday

long in the tooth old

mare female horse

mebbes not dialect for 'maybe not'

mounted sitting on a horse

muster gather

Non-Commissioned Officer (NCO) a soldier who has been promoted to the rank of Officer rather than appointed to it

out of sorts unwell, not your usual self

pit coal mine

Poppy Day 11th November, officially known as Remembrance Day; this marks the end of the First World War

prostrate lying horizontally, exhausted

shoring up propping up or making tunnels stable

snitch to tell on someone

strait narrow

taken the King's shilling agreed to fight as a soldier. The pay of a soldier used to be one shilling per day, which he was given when he signed up to the army, binding him in agreement

thick as thieves close friends

Titanic a legendary ocean liner that was meant to be unsinkable, but sank on its first voyage across the Atlantic when it struck an iceberg

trap a lightweight open carriage

walking out courting, going out as boyfriend and girlfriend

Wipers the British soldiers' joke name for Ypres, a town in Belgium